D0534719

D.I.Y. KIDS

ELLEN AND JULIA
LUPTON

NEW YORK
PRINCETON ARCHITECTURAL PRESS

**Thanks to all the kids
who contributed work:**

Asher
Ben
Danielle
Eliot
Eva
Graysen
Hannah
Hailey
Helen
Ilana
Isa
Isabel
Isabella
Isobel
Jay
Jean-Claude
Layla
Lucy
Marley
Mariah
Miriam
Nathalie
Orr
Rainer
Ronnie
Ruby
Sarah
Sydney
Tony
Tycho
Walker
Yen

**Thanks to the designers
who contributed projects
and interviews:**

Inna Alesina
Jen Bennett Gubizca
Joy Hayes
Marla Hollandsworth
Claire Joseph
Robert Lewis
Lynn Mally
Marilyn Milton
Ezri Tarazi

Thanks *to our parents for the "art box," the museum trips, and the encouragement. Thanks to our husbands for being great dads and helping clean up. Thanks to our friends and colleagues at Princeton Architectural Press; Maryland Institute College of Art; Cooper-Hewitt, National Design Museum; the University of California, Irvine; The Park School; and Tarbut v'Torah Community Day School.— Ellen and Julia Lupton*

Book Design: *Ellen Lupton*
Editing: *Clare Jacobson*
Typography: *Thesis type family, designed by Lucas de Groot*

Published by
Princeton Architectural Press
37 East Seventh Street
New York, New York 10003

For a free catalog of books, call 1.800.722.6657.
Visit our web site at www.papress.com.

© 2007 Princeton Architectural Press
All rights reserved
Printed and bound in China
10 09 08 07 5 4 3 2 1 First edition

No part of this book may be used or reproduced in any manner without written permission from the publisher, except in the context of reviews.

Every reasonable attempt has been made to identify owners of copyright. Errors or omissions will be corrected in subsequent editions.

Special thanks to: Nettie Aljian, Sara Bader, Dorothy Ball, Nicola Bednarek, Janet Behning, Becca Casbon, Penny (Yuen Pik) Chu, Russell Fernandez, Pete Fitzpatrick, Wendy Fuller, Jan Haux, John King, Mark Lamster, Nancy Eklund Later, Linda Lee, Katharine Myers, Lauren Nelson Packard, Jennifer Thompson, Arnoud Verhaeghe, Paul Wagner, Joseph Weston, and Deb Wood of Princeton Architectural Press—*Kevin C. Lippert, publisher*

Library of Congress Cataloging-in-Publication Data

Lupton, Ellen.
    D.I.Y. kids / Ellen and Julia Lupton.—1st ed.
        p. cm.
    Includes index.
    ISBN-13: 978-1-56898-707-1 (alk. paper)
    ISBN-10: 1-56898-707-2 (alk. paper)
    1. Handicraft—Juvenile literature. I. Lupton, Julia Reinhard, 1963- II. Title.
    TT160.L963 2007
    745.5—dc22

                                                                2007003397

CONTENTS

GRAPHICS

TOYS

HOME

FASHION

Reuse, recycle, remix!

Abandoned cereal boxes are an amazing material for art and design projects. They are easy to cut, and you can cover up their smooth gray insides quickly. In this book, you will find a castle, a magazine file, an art supply box, and other projects made out of cereal boxes. (We debranded the boxes with colored tape.)

Welcome to Our Book

How many cereal boxes does your family throw away each month? Who made all those boxes anyway, and what could *you* make with them?

Design is art people use. A graphic designer puts together words and pictures in order to create books, magazines, games, television graphics, Web sites, and other stuff you buy, see, and use. When you make your own cover for a school book report, or create a card for someone's birthday, you are a graphic designer, too.

Most of the art in this book was made by kids, ages 6–12. The art isn't as slick and perfect as what you see in glossy magazines or on flashy Web sites. Our book is a little rough and a little raw, and it's full of surprises, sparkle, and originality—just like kids.

Design is fun and functional. Use design to announce a yard sale, invite people to a party, or name your own band. Put your mark on T-shirts, magnets, bracelets, bags, book covers. Share your products with family and friends. Don't just buy or wear the brands you find at the store. Be your own brand, through the art of design. *—Ellen and Julia Lupton*

How much **help** will you need?

Try it alone. These projects require almost no help from an adult. (Even your four-year-old brother could do it.)

Get a little help. You might need a little help getting started, but even younger kids (ages 6–7) can get great results.

Get serious help. Now things are heating up! You may need help with cutting, hot glue, software, and other special techniques.

How much **time** will it take?

Quick trick. A quick project might take fifteen minutes or less. These activities are great for parties.

Relax and stay a while. Try these projects when you have at least half an hour to spare. Get comfortable, and get started.

Mark your calendar. A long project might take you all day, or you might start it on one afternoon and finish it the next.

How **messy** will it be?

Neat. These activities require only paper and a pencil or computer—pretty clean.

Pretty neat. These projects use paper, markers, scissors, or a little glue stick.

Messy. These projects use lots of glue—hot glue, wet glue—and you may have to haul out the fabric box or your watercolor set.

How much will it **cost**?

El Cheapo. As long as you have some paper, pencils, and markers, these are low-cost or no-cost activities.

A couple bucks. These activities involve decorating useful goods, from notebooks to T-shirts, or you may need special supplies.

Big bucks. Our high-end projects involve furniture. Decorating your room the D.I.Y. way is still cheaper than fancy shopping.

Find these symbols underneath each project.
We've included an index of projects at the back of the book.

How much help will you need?

Office Dot Buddy, p. 12

Circle Skirt, p. 70

Stuffed Animal, p. 76

How much time will it take?

Altered Notebook, p. 60

Fluffy Cup Cozy, p. 106

Zine Box, p. 92

How messy will it be?

Hand-Drawn Pattern, p. 27

Clothespin Dolls, p. 66

Decoupage Purse, p. 122

How much will it cost?

Fashion Sketching, p. 114

Transfer Shirt, p. 125

Arty Art Table, p. 89

Graphic designers create logos, magazines, books, Web sites, CD covers, and many other media that you see and read every day. They put together words and pictures to get ideas across to people. Robert Lewis is a graphic designer who lives in Washington, D.C. He is starting his own magazine, called *Allawe*, devoted to art and culture in the Caribbean.

When did you decide to become a designer?
In college, I was interested in the sciences, but I had always loved art. I happened to take an illustration class taught by a graphic designer, and that's when I discovered what I really wanted to do.

What did you make when you were a kid?
I liked creating necklaces and keychains. I also made book bags from old curtains and cloth I found around the house, and I sold the bags at school.

What is your dream project?
Growing up in Trinidad, I wasn't encouraged to become a visual artist. Through Allawe *magazine, I hope to celebrate the creative environment that exists in the Caribbean and change Caribbean people's perception of careers in the arts.*

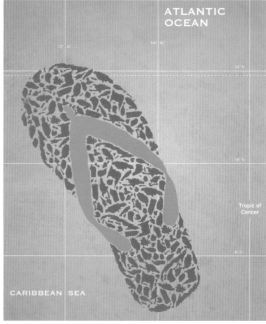

GRAPHICS

Characters

A character is a made-up creature with quirky features and a memorable personality. Mickey Mouse and Hello Kitty have simple features that instantly say who they are. A character can be cute, sassy, silly, or just plain evil. It can be an animal, vegetable, alien, or the lady next door. Give your character huge eyes, pointy ears, or a funny color. Make it by hand or build it on the computer.

When you've designed a great character, draw it on your notebooks, sign your name with it, or put it on T-shirts, tote bags, or pencil boxes. Make one great character, or build a whole army!

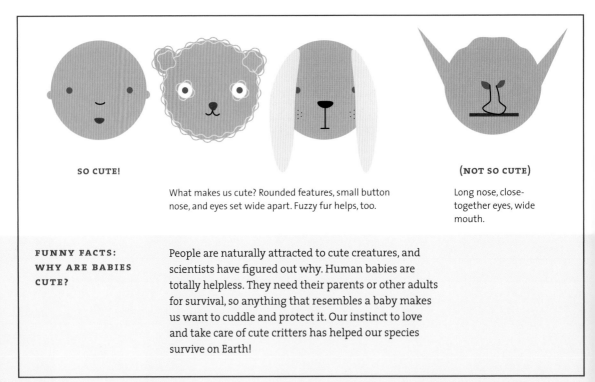

SO CUTE!

What makes us cute? Rounded features, small button nose, and eyes set wide apart. Fuzzy fur helps, too.

(NOT SO CUTE)

Long nose, close-together eyes, wide mouth.

FUNNY FACTS: WHY ARE BABIES CUTE?

People are naturally attracted to cute creatures, and scientists have figured out why. Human babies are totally helpless. They need their parents or other adults for survival, so anything that resembles a baby makes us want to cuddle and protect it. Our instinct to love and take care of cute critters has helped our species survive on Earth!

1. Make a head. Draw it by hand or on the computer, or use office dots, foam pieces, tape, or cut paper.

2. Add eyes and mouth. You can do it with just a hint: a moustache or a beak makes a mouth, and two circles or slits become eyes.

Teddy Boy   **Big Mouth**   **Flat Top**

3. Name your character.

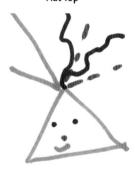

Grape Girl   **French Freda**   **Volcano Val**

Designed by Ruby, Hannah, and Jay, ages 7–11

Flow Pow   **Block Head**   **Hot Bot**

Use plain round stickers to make heads, bodies, and more. Add details with tape and markers.

Designed by Eliot, Hannah, Ronnie, and Jay, ages 6–11

COOL!
Stick your office dot buddies on notebooks, gift wrap, and more.

The Tantrum
Make a scene with office dots
and colored tape. *Designed by
Ronnie, age 9*

Lieutenant Glue

Captain Sheet

General Ruler

Sargeant Staple Remover

Private Paper Clip

Colonel Pencil

Major Mug

Corporal
Scissors

Imagine if objects could come to life. Where would the face go, and where is the body?

Office Warriors
Designed by Jay, age 11

DUST BUNNIES

MORE IDEAS
Dust bunnies live under your bed! Get ideas from the funny ways we describe the world. What would these characters look like?
- *Cheap Skate*
- *Fat Cat*
- *Dream Boat*
- *Sweet Pea*

Dust Bunny
This character has its very own font. *Designed by Hannah, age 9*

> **HEY!**
> Merchandise with your own characters makes great gifts.

You can personalize all kinds of objects with your own characters. Draw them on cotton purses or tote bags.

Cover a leftover box with paper or colored tape. Draw your characters on the box, and use it for storing pencils, toys, gifts, etc.

Animal Friends
The polka dots make a pretty background for characters inspired by favorite stuffed animals.
Designed by Ruby, age 7

Savage Pillow
Designed by Jay, age 11

1. Get a "pillow form" or an old pillow (medium-sized, 16 x 16 inches). A pillow form is a plain pillow with a papery outside.

2. Get a standard bedroom pillow case. Fold the case around the pillow. Mark with pins or little dots where your drawing area will be.

3. Take the case off the pillow and draw on it with Sharpies or fabric markers.

4. Put the pillow back in the case and stitch it shut.

TIP You can't really wash this pillow, but by the time it gets dirty, you'll want to make a new one.

Icons

An icon is a simple picture that is easy to see and understand. It expresses an idea without any words. Many computer programs use icons (magnifying glass, scissors, pen, pencil, folder, and so on). Signs on bathrooms and airports use icons to show people where to go (and where to "go"). Draw your own icons to put on your computer desktop in place of standard folders. Make your own IM buddy icons, or just draw cool icons on your stuff.

Computer Icons
Use your own icons to personalize your instant messaging account and the folders on your computer desktop.

Designed by Hannah and Jay, ages 9 and 11

Cupcake Icons
Tasty little cupcakes make a sweet pattern for stationery, wrapping paper, or a T-shirt.
Designed by Ruby, Sydney, and Rainer, ages 7–10

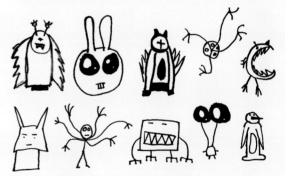

GET IT?

We created these icons to describe the projects in this book. Can you guess what they mean? (See key on page 6.)

Icons designed by Lucy, Ruby, and Jay, ages 6–11

SO CUTE!
Tiny drawings are adorable. (These are printed actual size.)

Make icons about a single subject: food, clothes, hair, aliens, etc. Or, just fill in a grid of little stickers with random stuff; what ties them together is their tiny size.

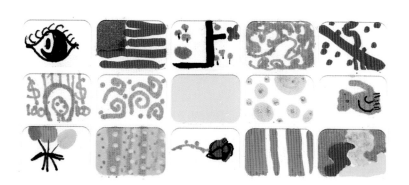

"Pixel art" is a style of digital drawing that uses pixel blocks instead of smooth lines. Pixel art has become its own visual style, with simple, blocky forms. Think of pixel art as drawing with Legos! If you have some basic Photoshop skills, you can build a collection of pixel icons. Make them with friends and share them. These hard-core, low-res dudes make great buddy icons.
Designed by Jay, age 11

New York City Poster
Our pixel icons are inspired by the work of eBoy, a team of digital designers who have created a huge collection of pixel people, objects, building parts, and more. The eBoy design team builds detailed landscapes and pictures with their pixel collection. *Designed by eBoy. See more at www.eboy.com.*

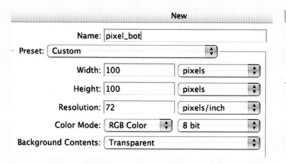

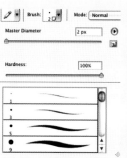

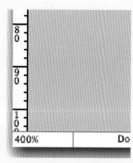

NERD ALERT!
This project requires some basic Photoshop knowledge.

1. Open a new file in Photoshop. Make the file 100 x 100 pixels, 72 pixels per inch. Make it transparent.

2. Select the pencil tool and make its diameter 2 pixels, and make its hardness 100%.

3. With the magnifying glass, blow up the image on your screen to 400%. This will make your pencil match the gray and white squares in the background.

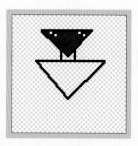

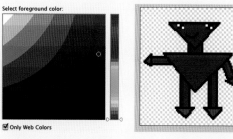

4. Start drawing. Every time you click on the screen, a single square will appear. The background grid will help you with your design. To make a straight line, hold down the shift key while you draw. Fill in solid areas with the paint bucket.

5. Add shading to make your drawing really pop. Open the color picker window and choose a shade darker than your main color. Make highlights the same way: in the color picker, choose a shade lighter than your basic color.

6. Draw a line along the edge of your shape.

Logos

A logo is an interesting way to write the name of a person, product, school, band, etc. Even little kids who don't know how to read can recognize lots of logos (McDonald's, Dunkin' Donuts, Toys "R" Us). Make a logo to put on your stuff or to promote your own music or art. You can make it on the computer or draw it by hand.

ASHER INC.

Monogram Logo
This logo is a kid's initials (AZS), drawn on the computer in Flash. He uses it on T-shirts, notebooks, stickers, and other stuff. *Designed by Asher, age 11*

Blue Dude Films
A young filmmaker designed this logo for his movie company and made shirts to raise money for his productions. He sold dozens of shirts at his junior high school in Santa Monica, California. *Designed by Tycho, age 13*

Cheesy Camp Logo
We designed this logo for a week at home. We put it on T-shirts and notebooks, and enjoyed not going anywhere. *Designed by Hannah, age 9*

snıper rıfle

Box Cuttar

Mĕdiă Săvăgĕ

Band Logos
*Designed by Jay, Jean-Claude,
and Walker, ages 11–13*

Sugar Rush CD Cover
Designed by Jay, age 11

Death Valley Girls CD Label
These graphics are drawn
directly on a plain CD label.
Designed by Hannah, age 9

Band Logos

Do you have a band, or do you just want to have one? Real or not, every band needs a cool name and a cool way to write it.

1. Think of interesting words or phrases. The band names we came up with all sound a little bit dangerous or weird.

2. Choose a phrase you like and try writing it in an interesting way.

3. Put your logo on gear for your band: CDs, T-shirts, and stickers. Write it on your notebook, your shoes, your hoodie, or your denim jacket. A lot of the projects in this book make handy band merchandise.

Patterns

Patterns are one of the oldest forms of decoration. A pattern is a design that uses the same elements over and over. Use anything to make a pattern: dots, stripes, or cherry pie! A pattern can be perfectly regular (like a checkerboard) or scattered (like leaves on the ground).

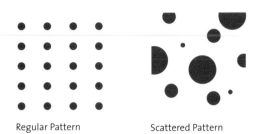

Regular Pattern   Scattered Pattern

Hand-Drawn Patterns
Draw a shape or object over and over. Fill in the areas in between with different shapes.

Sweet Stuff Tote
Draw patterns with Sharpie on a cotton tote bag.
Designed by Ruby, age 7

*Patterns designed by Ruby,
Hannah, and Isabel, ages 6–9*

Make patterns by repeating words on a page. Use your handwritten pattern for a card or wrapping paper, or scan it and add additional images or color in a program such as Photoshop.

Twelve Little Monkeys
Monkey heads inspired by Paul Frank sit on top of scribbled words. This image was drawn by hand on one surface. *Designed by Ronnie, age 9*

Hi Hi Hi

The letters were drawn with a Sharpie pen. Then we scanned them and used the pattern in a lot of projects shown in this book. To make the graphics for the T-shirt and zine box, we added large decorated letters.
Designed by Hannah, age 9

MAKE IT!
Find out how to make this zine box on page 92

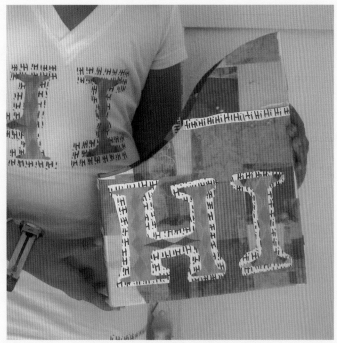

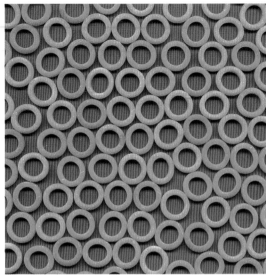

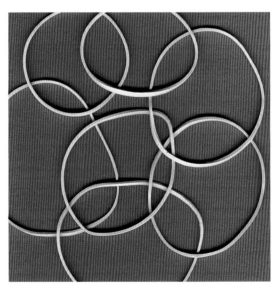

Use your scanner to make pictures of small flat objects. We tried pasta, rubber bands, ribbons, coins, and leaves. Lay objects on the scanner glass (or on a photocopier). For best results, don't let objects overlap too much (keep your stuff in one flat layer). When you like the arrangement, put a sheet of colored paper on top. Scan or copy! Use your scans for wrapping paper, book covers, decoupage, and other projects. *Never* put wet, sticky, or sharp objects on the scanner or copier glass.

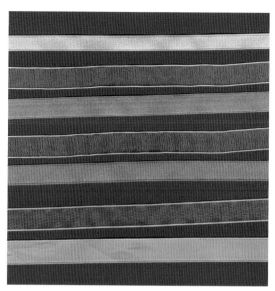

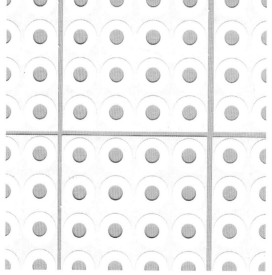

Checkerboard Pattern

Most patterns that you see on wrapping paper or fabric are repeating patterns. Computers are great for making repeating patterns with drawings that you like, or just with colors and shapes. You can use many different software programs to make repeating patterns, including Word and Photoshop.

GEEK METER!
This project will test your computer skills (and your patience).

1. Scan pictures or draw them on the computer. Make your pictures all the same size. (Ours are 200 x 280 pixels). We gave our pictures different background colors.

2. Create a table in Word. (Ours is four columns and four rows.) Select "AutoFit to contents" for behavior. This makes the cells the same size as your pictures.

3. Insert pictures into each cell. Make a repeating pattern with your drawings.

You can also do this project in Photoshop by copying and pasting your pictures into one file. (Make them all one size first.)

MORE IDEAS
- Make wrapping paper for small gifts.
- Fold patterned paper in half for a note card.
- Add a message to make a greeting card.
- Glue your pattern to a wooden or cardboard box.
- Use your pattern as a background for a scrapbook page.

Flik and Her Friends
To make this checkerboard pattern, we scanned six drawings and added the background colors in Photoshop. We made the pictures all one size and put them in a table in Word. *Designed by Hannah, Ronnie, and Orr, age 9*

Some patterns that look irregular are actually made by a machine or a computer, and they copy the same elements. This is called a *random repeat*. Many wallpaper and fabric designs look irregular, but they're not!

Random repeats are built out of "tiles." The edges of every tile have to match up with the edges of other tiles, but the stuff inside can be anywhere. To make this repeat pattern in Photoshop, we made a new file (transparent) and copied and pasted the eyeball guy a few times. We arranged the copies inside a rectangular area in the middle of the page (our "tile"). Four guys overlap the edges of the tile. We copied the tile area and made the guys overlap to create a perfect pattern.

NERD ALERT!
This project takes some computer savvy to work out.

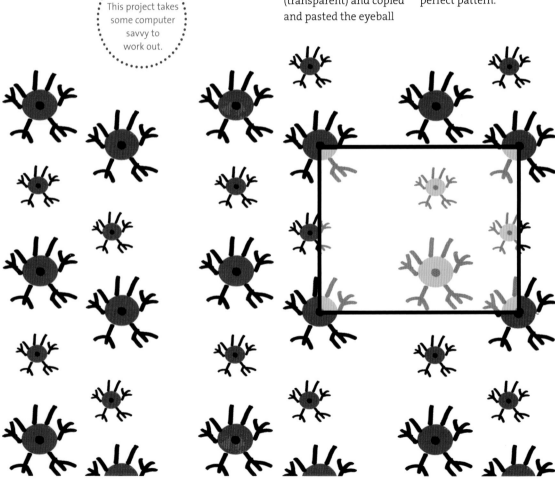

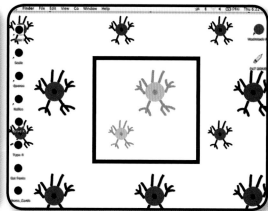

If your Photoshop skills are on the minimal side, try this quick experiment with your desktop.

1. Make a little drawing in Photoshop, and choose it for the desktop of your computer. Set the desktop to "tile."

2. Try it with different pictures. Some will look super-regular, like a chess board. Try to get a random-looking effect.

3. Like your design? Take a "screen shot"! ("Command-shift-4" on a Mac; "Control-shift-4" on a PC.)

Random Eyeball
Deck out your desktops (your real one and the one on your screen) with your own pattern designs. Kits for making iron-on mouse pads are available at office supply stores, or you can have one made through an on-line service such as CafePress.com. *Eyeball graphic designed by Eliot, age 6*

Lettering

Like people, letters come in many sizes, shapes, colors, and styles. It's amazing how much you can play around with the basic shape of a letter, and still be able to read it. Make your letters fancy, fuzzy, or 3-D. Use your own letters to make logos and titles for your books and magazines, or to write your name on your stuff.

Freaky, Funny Letters
Pick a descriptive word: stinky, slimy, swirly, bright. Create letters that look like your word.

Designed by Ruby, Hannah, Jay, and Tony, ages 7–11

Fancy, Wacky Letters

A letter can look like a thing. Use bumblebees to make a *B*, or use an *S* to make a snake. Set a bowl of fruit on top of the letter *F*.

Letters can be made of fancy shapes and lots of colors. Make curly letters, outline letters, polka dot letters, and more. Make cool numbers and punctuation, too.

Designed by Ruby, age 7

Stickers

It's fun to draw on stickers. Get inspired by the special shapes and sizes of mailing labels, tiny price tags, and office dots. Make a cartoon on a sheet of square labels, or make funny faces on a sheet of round ones. Stickers can be useful, too. Create a bookplate for a special gift, decorate goody bags for a party, or adorn a wrapped present with them.

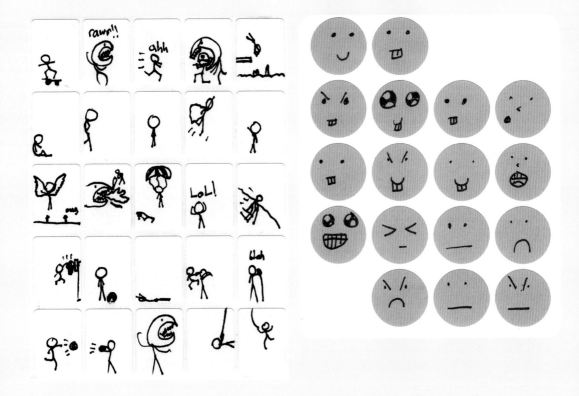

Sticker Art

Use a sheet of tiny stickers to create a collection of purses, cakes, or monsters. Draw inside the bright printed frame of a mailing label.

Postal Stickers

Design your own stamps for make-believe mail.

Stickers designed by Ruby, Isabella, Isobel, and Jay, ages 7–11

Bookplate Stickers

A bookplate is a sticker that goes inside a book. It usually says who owns the book, and it can also say who gave the book as a gift. Make bookplates to go inside your own homemade books, inside your notebook, or inside a special present (such as a book for a teacher or a new baby). Make one-of-a-kind bookplates or photocopy your favorites.

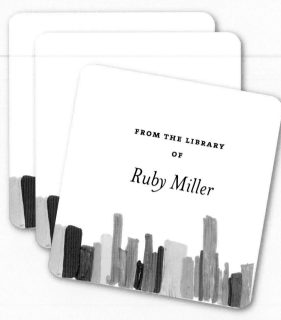

TIPS • If you are putting a bookplate in an important book, make sure you use an archival (acid-free) glue or library paste. • To print on label paper, use a template that comes with Word. Insert your design into the label squares. • Make your own archival stickers with a Xyron sticker-maker.

Personalized Bookplates
A stack of bookplates makes a great gift. Scan a drawing and add type on the computer. Print them on office labels, or print them on sheets of sticky paper and cut them out by hand.

Paintings by Isabel and Ruby, ages 6 and 7

SEW COOL!
Look closely to see where this book was sewn together.

Scan your bookplate and add a border and type.

Watercolor Bookplates

1. Draw a rectangle on a sheet of drawing paper or watercolor paper. (Tracing around a note card is fast and accurate.)

2. In pencil, draw outlines of book spines. (Use a ruler, or just draw freehand.)

3. Color in the spines with watercolor. It's pretty how the colors mix around a little.

4. When the paint is dry, add words and decorations with a black pen.

5. If you like, scan your design and add text or a box for writing a message. Print as many copies as you want.

6. Cut out around the rectangle, and use library paste or a photo-quality glue stick to attach the plate to your book.

Designed by Isabel, Eliot, and Ronnie, ages 6–9

Cards

Send a message with your own graphic style. Homemade cards and invitations are a personal way to say "Hello," "Thank you," or "Please come to my party." Make them by hand, print them from a computer, or send them by e-mail.

Celebrate with us!   Ruby's house

Saturday, July 1   RSVP 410-555-1212
12:00–4:00pm   ruby@gmail.com

PARTY

When	Saturday, July 1, 12:00–4:00pm
What	Paint a still life* on real canvas
Where	Ruby's house
Wear	An old T-shirt or smock
Bring	A simple object to paint
RSVP	410-555-1212, ruby@gmail.com

*A still life is a painting of objects.

Party Fliers
The easiest way to produce your own invitation is to print out a flyer on standard printer paper. Scan in your own special lettering or graphics.

Happy Letters
The handmade lettering makes this super-simple invitation special. We scanned the lettering and then did the rest of the text on the computer. *Lettering by Ruby, age 7*

Stamp Art
We used rubber stamps to make the main lettering and then added decorations with markers. We scanned the decorated lettering and then did the rest of the text on the computer. *Lettering by Ruby, age 7*

COME TO OUR
STUFFED ANIMAL PARTY

RUBY'S HOUSE
WEDS, JULY 5, 1:00 PM

BRING YOUR FAVORITE
STUFFED ANIMAL

MAKE ANIMAL TAGS,
ANIMAL BLANKETS, AND OTHER
FUN STUFF WITH US

Print-and-Fold Invitation

If you want to print out a bunch of invitations, try this simple print-and-fold design.

Cover graphic by Ruby, age 7

Put your cover design and your inside text on the same side of the paper, but put the text upside down, as shown on the picture on the left. Fold the paper in half, and then half again, to get a sweet little card.

From: Ellen Lupton <elupton@designwritingresearch.org>   To: Ellen Lupton <elupton@des
Subject: Stuffed Animal Party
Attachments: doggy_eVite.jpg

doggy_eVite.jpg

Come to Our Stuffed Animal Party.

Ruby's House
Weds, July 5, 1:00pm

Bring your favorite stuffed animal.

Make animal tags, animal blankets, and other fun stuff.

COME TO OUR STUFFED ANIMAL PARTY

RUBY'S HOUSE
WEDS, JULY 5, 1:00 PM

BRING YOUR FAVORITE STUFFED ANIMAL

MAKE ANIMAL TAGS,
ANIMAL BLANKETS, AND
OTHER FUN STUFF WITH US

E-mail Invitation

You'd rather go digital? No problem. Scan your picture or draw one in Photoshop. Add room around your picture for the text by making the canvas size bigger in Photoshop (Image>Canvas Size). Our canvas is 600 x 300 px. Type in your text.

Always include the important information in the text of your e-mail, too, because some people might have trouble seeing your picture file, depending on how their computer works.

Pop-up cards are a fun and dramatic way to send a message. The best pop-ups tell a story. On this card, the sleeping cat on the cover "wakes up" when you open the card. On your card, will a flower bloom? A cloud burst into thunder? A firecracker explode? Does your card share a riddle or two parts of a rhyme?

You can use elements from clip art, magazines, comic books, digital photos, or your own drawings. Words can also pop-up. (Don't forget punctuation!)

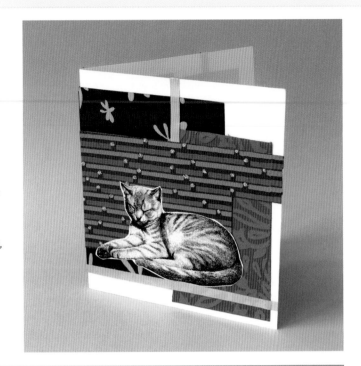

Wake the Kitty
This card uses one piece of card stock covered with fancy paper and some colored tape. A long piece of fancy paper wraps front to back, covering the hole made by the pop-up cutaway. Black and white clip art stands out against the colorful background. *Designed by Hannah, age 9*

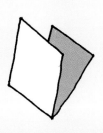

1. Fold a sheet of card stock in half.

2. At the fold, cut two slits two inches long.

3. Fold the slit away from the card fold, making a firm crease. If you've cut and folded the card correctly, an empty rectangle will appear along the fold.

4. Open the card.

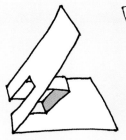

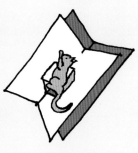

5. Carefully pull out the folded "tongue."

6. Fold the card so that the tongue lies flat, away from the card's central fold.

7. Attach your pop-up image to the top surface of the tongue. Before gluing your pop-up image down, make sure that the card can close without bending the pop-up, and without having any piece of the pop-up stick out from the other side.

8. Glue a second folded piece of card stock to the outside. This will be the front and back of your card. Make sure you don't get glue inside the open area left by the cut-out tongue. You can add writing or additional pictures around the pop-up.

TIPS ● Making more than one? Photocopy the cover, the inside, and the pop-up on separate sheets of cardstock. Include cut marks for the pop-up tongue to make cutting easier. ● To put more than one pop-up in the same card, just cut extra slits, and make sure your images are small enough to fit inside the card.

Take black-and-white pictures of old engravings from clip art books (we like Dover Books), old-fashioned paper doll books, or photocopies from art books. Use watercolors or colored pencils to add color to the drawings.

Then cut out the figures and glue them onto folded card stock. If you want, you can preprint the card stock with greetings or party information.

Wedding Shower
To make this card for a wedding shower, we printed out the bride-to-be's name on card stock and then added hand-colored collage elements. *Wedding cards designed by Hannah, age 9*

Modern Collage

For a different look, keep the engravings black-and-white, and then paste the cut-out figures onto bright patterned paper.

The contrast between the old-fashioned black-and-whites and the contemporary patterns looks sharp. Colored tape adds another crisp accent. *Kitty cards designed by Jay and Hannah, ages 9 and 11*

Book Arts

Create beautiful blank books to sketch and write in, or make casual zines about fashion or sports. Handmade books are great for scrapbooking— fill them with special pictures and artwork. Books make wonderful gifts, too.

SEW COOL!
The book you're reading was sewn, too. Find the stitches, p. 40

Sewn Books

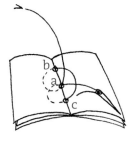

1. Get a stack of 4–8 sheets of plain paper plus one sheet of card stock. Fold the paper and card stock carefully in half. (Folding each sheet separately can get neater results.)

2. With a hammer and a small nail or push pin, gently poke three holes in the center of the book. Be sure to go through all the pages at once.

3. Thread a needle and pull it down through the center hole from inside the book (a). Then push the needle through an outside hole (b), and then back through the last hole (c). Finally, pull it up through the middle hole again (a).

4. Tie the threads together in a knot. Be sure to leave enough thread to tie; adjust the threads if you didn't. Use tape, stickers, labels, and fancy paper to decorate your book. This style of book binding is called the *pamphlet stitch*.

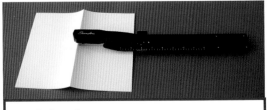

Stapled Books
For a fast alternative, use a long-necked stapler instead of needle and thread!

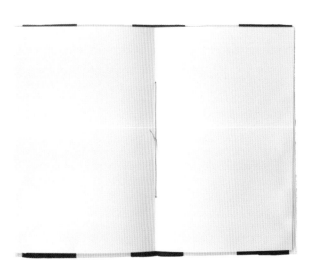

Cut a piece of fabric a little bigger than your sheet of card stock. Attach it to the card stock with double-stick tape all around the edges. (You can also use a special glue called PVA, designed for bookbinding.) Follow the directions for a sewn book at left, sewing through both the cloth cover and the pages inside. Decorate with beads, felt pockets, ribbons, and patches.

Designed by Ruby and Isabella, ages 7 and 8

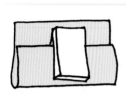

1. Get a mini notepad. Cut fabric about 2 1/2 times the pad's width, and 1 1/2 times its height. Fold the fabric over the cardboard backing of the pad and mark the crease with a pencil.

2. Unfold the flap, and apply three lines of hot glue to make pockets for the pad and for supplies. Be sure to leave enough room for the pad to fit in the pocket.

3. Press the flap down over the glue, and insert the pad into the pocket.

4. Fold the side flap and the cover around the pad.

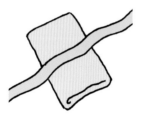

5. Turn the package with its folds down and apply a line of hot glue along the middle.

6. Press a piece of ribbon or trim into the hot glue.

7. Put markers or other supplies in the left pocket.

8. Fold it back up, tie the whole thing shut, and you're good to go!

TIPS ● A standard sheet of felt works well with this project, requiring very little cutting and waste. Fleece works, too, because it doesn't fray. ● For a tougher look, use an old pair of jeans or an old leather jacket. ● You can make this project out of heavy paper instead of fabric.

Fluffy Notepad Holders
Designed by Ruby, Isobel, and Isabella, ages 7–8

Zines are simple homemade magazines. They can be made by hand, with a photocopier, or on a computer. Adults make zines about many topics (from music and art to their favorite TV shows), and they sell or give away their zines to other zinesters. The zines shown here were made by hand using stapled pages.

Montage Zine
This zine is made by cutting and pasting old-fashioned pictures. You can get funny effects by overlapping pieces or cutting them into odd shapes. *Designed by Lucy, age 6*

America Girl
This fashion zine features fancy dresses and an ad for sushi. *Designed by Ruby and Isabella, ages 7 and 8*

Scrapbooks are a great way to record a trip or a special birthday, idolize your pets, or package a book report. Keep your scrapbooks for yourself or give them away as gifts. Small scrapbooks made of low-cost materials are great: you can fill them up fast, and then you can make more books on different subjects and for different audiences.

?!?! ⊘⊘⊘ ✹ ✹ ⓢⓢ

My Book of Cats
These scrapbooks use photos of our cats and our own object patterns for backgrounds (see page 30). Additional accents include office dots, notebook hole labels, skinny colored masking tape, and kitty clip art. *Designed by Lucy and Hannah, ages 6 and 9*

Recycle old board books by making them into albums. The cardboard pages withstand heavy gluing. You can paint over the original artwork with white gesso primer or let the original drawings show through, adding accidental content to your pages.

To document a special trip, collect matchbooks, business cards, tickets, hotel give-aways— even your vacation homework! Make labels on the computer or write on office dots and colored masking tape.

Designed by Hannah, age 9

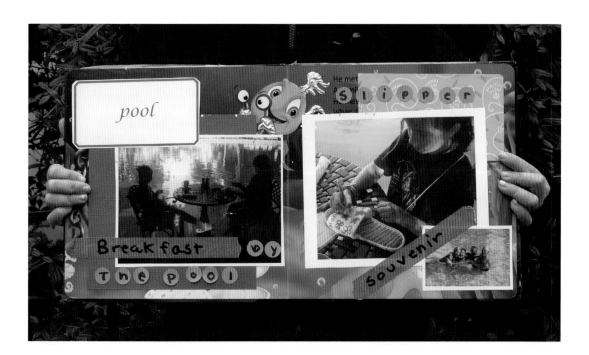

The popular Ologies books (Candlewick Press) inspired this book project. Choose a fanciful subject (pirates, unicorns, monsters, aliens) and create 3-D pages using envelopes, pop-ups, fold-outs, and other add-ons. You can "age" your inserts by tearing the edges and staining them with watercolor.

Pirates
This page features drawings made right on the page, with torn-paper additions glued on. *Designed by Jay, age 11*

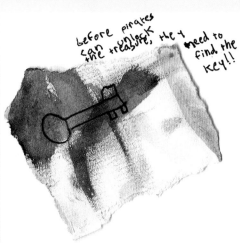

Pirate 2
This page features a tiny book, a treasure map, and some treasure. Pieces of fabric and glitter glue add extra texture and sparkle. *Designed by Hannah, age 9*

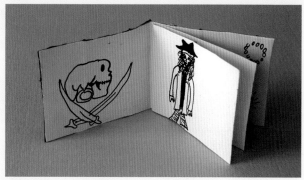

Why write or draw in a boring notebook, when it's fun and easy to make it all your own? Glue interesting pictures onto a standard-issue notebook. Use stickers, tape, office dots, markers, and more to build your own cover design.

WOW!
Altered notebooks are a fun and easy party activity.

Sticker and Tape Notebooks
Make lettering and decora–tions with skinny tape. Glue on drawings or make characters with office dots.

Designed by Hannah and Jay, ages 9 and 11

Caterpillar and Kapow!
We used black-and-white clip art and colored it by hand. *Designed by Isabel and Mariah, ages 6 and 10*

Cut-Out Notebook Covers
Cut a window in the cover of a notebook with an X-Acto knife. (Ask an adult to help with the cutting.) Paste a picture on the first page, so that you can see it through the window.

Toy designers create games, dolls, stuffed animals, and other fun things to play with. Jen Bennett Gubzica works for a graphic design company called Big Blue Dot in Boston, where she recently designed packaging for an action figure called Naruto. She also makes her own line of handmade stuffed animals, which she sells on line.

When did you decide to become a designer?

I was always interested in art as a kid. When I was seventeen, I did an internship with Big Blue Dot, a design studio dedicated to kids and families. I fell in love with design and chose that as my major when I went to college.

What did you make when you were a kid?

I used to draw a lot. I made large posters for my siblings, cousins, and friends to hang in their rooms. My mother and I made a stuffed cat as a baby gift for a neighbor, so that was my first stuffed animal.

What is your dream project?

I would love to travel to other countries, researching character and toy design.

TOYS

Primitive Toys

A toy can be as simple as a rock, a paper plate, or your finger with a face drawn on it. When you're stuck in a restaurant or on an airplane, make toys out of the stuff around you. With primitive toys, the fun often comes with the number: make a whole army of aliens, ballerinas, or eye ball monsters.

Ketchup Dolls
Use markers to create faces on the back of ketchup tubes. When you're done, "kill" them and watch the blood come out (if your parents don't mind the mess).

Marshmallow Guys

Simple craft "marsh-mallows" (available from craft stores) come alive when you stick push pins into them to make arms, legs, eyes, and other features.

Sock Dolls

Fill old socks with sand, tie with rubber bands, and give them faces. These are great toys to make and play with at the park or beach.

Primitive toys designed by Hannah, Ronnie, Isabel, Lucy, and Eliot, ages 6–9

Wooden clothespins make great mannequins for designing miniature fashions. Gather up scraps of fabric, ribbon, lace, yarn, and fancy paper, and put together outfits that are fun and fabulous.

You can use ordinary clothespins, or you can buy special ones from a craft store that have little wooden bases for the dolls to stand on.

Hot glue is the fastest way to attach the elements. (Careful, please!) You can also sew them or use school glue.

Attach the fabrics directly to the wood, or glue only fabric-to-fabric so that your outfits can come on and off the mannequin dolls.

Designed by Hannah, age 9

Fashion Sketching
Sketch your fashions when you're done or draw designs you'd like to make.

Spring Collection
This awesome lineup was made by a group of girls at an art party.

Designed by Hannah, Helen, Nathalie, Ruby, and Isobel, ages 7–9

Fashion for Toys

Go wild with your dolls and make-believe pets, and create special jewelry and clothing that's all your own. Experiment with materials, colors, and trimmings.

Animal Tags

At a craft store or hardware store, you can get little paper tags with a metal rim (normally used for identifying keys and for scrapbooking).

These sturdy little medallions make great tags for your stuffed animals. (The plain white ones work best.) Write your creature's name, draw a picture, make up a phone number, invent a secret icon. Tie on the tag with a piece of ribbon or yarn.

Designed by Ruby, age 8

Tag Necklace

Paper tags make great necklaces, too. *Designed by Isabel, age 6*

MORE IDEAS While you are making tags for your favorite stuffed critters, try these fun activities, too. • Add a leash with a long piece of ribbon. • Create ID cards, drivers' licenses, or passports. • Design birth certificates, hospital records, and diet and exercise programs.

Crazy Beautiful
This handmade bunny head is finished off with an animal tag. *Designed by Lucy, age 6*

Circle Skirts

These simple skirts are inspired by the work of Italian fashion designer Miuccia Prada, who thinks that skirts are the most creative and comfortable kind of women's clothing. Whether you like wearing skirts or not, your dolls and animals will love them.

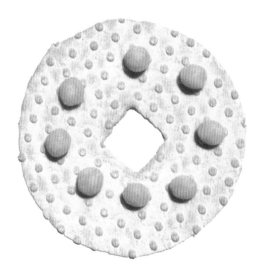

1. Find a round object like a plate or a roll of tape. Use it to trace a circle on a piece of fabric. We like fleece because it doesn't unravel, but you can try other fabrics, too. The bigger the circle, the longer the skirt, so experiment to find a size that fits your toy.

2. Fold the circle in half and in half again, making a rounded triangle. Cut off the very top of the triangle to make the waist opening in the skirt. Make a tiny hole to start with. Because you are cutting through several layers of fabric, the hole will be bigger than you think!

3. Try the skirt on your toy, and make the hole bigger if you need to.

4. Decorate the skirt with fancy trim. (We used hot glue.)

Designed by Isobel, Ruby, and Hailey, ages 7–8

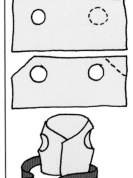

Rectangle Vest

1. Cut a rectangle big enough to wrap around your toy. Cut out one arm hole and try vest on toy.

2. Wrap fabric around toy and cut second hole.

3. Angle the neck line, and glue on a piece of ribbon for a sash.

?! ?! ◷ ◷ ⬤ ⬤ ⓢ ⓢ

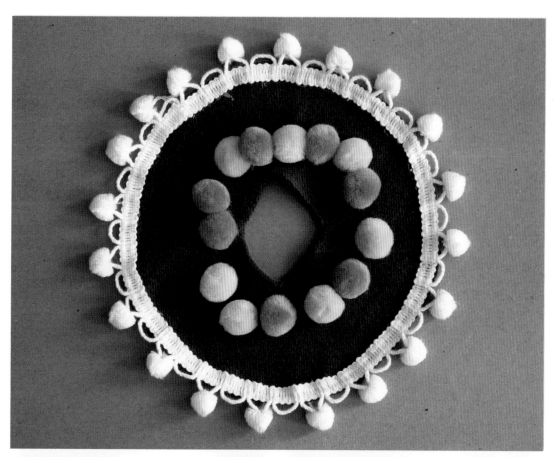

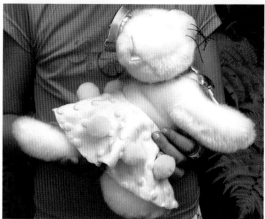

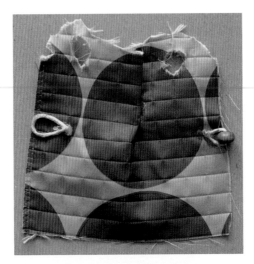

Fitted Coat-Vest
This long coat-vest has a working button made by hot-gluing some string and a bead to the fabric. The button lets Barbie take her coat off to reveal the matching sleeveless dress underneath. To make the coat fit well on Barbie's hourglass figure, make a dart in the back by pinching the fabric and gluing it in place. *Designed by Helen, age 8*

Barbie Clothes
Even if you're getting too old to play with Barbies and other mannequin dolls, it's fun to design clothes for them. It takes only a tiny bit of fabric to make an outfit. It's challenging to make clothes for Barbie that actually come on and off, because her hips are so much wider than her waist. The dress shown here is semipermanent, but the vest comes off.

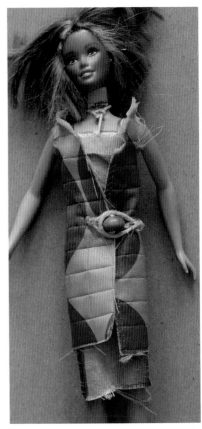

Polly Pocket Clothes

Polly Pocket dolls are easy to make clothes for. Unlike Barbie, Polly has tiny hips and a small chest, so you can make clothes that slide on and off her. (The toy company had this in mind when they designed Polly's cute figure; her rubber outfits don't have any buttons or zippers, either.)

Experiment with dresses, tops, skirts, and even pants. Add lace and trim.

Designed by Layla, Ruby, Eva, and Isabella, ages 5–9

Stuffed Animals

Project designed by Jen Bennett Gubicza

Think about your favorite stuffed toy. Why do you love it? Was it your first one? Is it soft and cuddly? A gift from someone special? Using these basic instructions, you can design your own stuffed animal. Starting from a simple circle, invent a creature with eyes, nose, ears, and more.

Getting Started

This project takes some time to complete, and younger kids will need help with cutting fabric, threading needles, and tying knots.

The best fabric for this project is fleece, which is soft and cozy and won't unravel when you cut it. Buy some at a fabric store, or recycle an old sweater or baby blanket.

You will also need needles, thread, pins, scissors, and fuzzy stuffing. (You can buy pillow stuffing, or use soft fabric scraps.) If you are having a party or working with a group, it helps to cut out some basic shapes before you start, so everyone can have fun designing with the shapes and colors without worrying about too much cutting.

Designing Your Stuffy

Start with a basic circle. Is the circle a head or a body? Will your creature have eyes and ears, legs and arms? Check out our ideas on the next three pages.

Draw your design on paper, or play around with precut circles and squares of fabric. When you are happy with your design, you are ready to start sewing.

Floppy Puppy

This basic stuffy is a big circle with long floppy ears. The eyes and nose are circles of dark fabric stitched on to the face (called appliqué). The mouth is sewn with black thread (embroidered). This toy also makes a great little pillow.

?! ?! ?! ⊕⊕⊕ 🐾🐾 ⓓⓓ

Making Your Stuffy

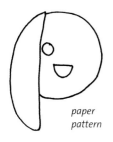  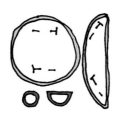 

paper pattern

1. Make a paper pattern. To make a circle, trace a round object, like a cup or plate. Boxes or baking pans are good for tracing rectangles.

2. Pin your pattern. Pin through two layers of fabric to make two matching pieces at once. The puppy's ears are green inside and blue outside, so you'll need four pieces altogether.

3. Cut around the pattern and through the fabric. To make matching ears, flip the pattern over to make the second ear.

4. Now, pin the fabric together to make the ears. Some fleece has a "wrong" and "right" side. (The right side might be fluffier or have a pattern on it.) Pin the fabric with the wrong side facing in.

 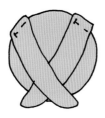 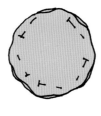 

5. Sew both ears first. Leave an opening where the ear will meet the head. Use neat, tiny stitches so the stuffing won't fall out. Carefully turn the ear inside out and add a little stuffing if you want.

6. When you have both ears sewn, lay one of your big circles down with the right side up, and arrange your ears on top of the circle. Pin them all in place.

7. Now, pin the other big circle on top, wrong side up, making a giant ravioli. (The ears will be *inside* the ravioli.) Sew around the ravioli, leaving an opening at the bottom. When you get to the thick part where the ears get sewn in, make sure to go through all the fabric. Stitch these parts twice for extra strength.

8. Turn your stuffie inside out, like a sweater. Amazing! There's your creature with its ears magically connected at the seams. Gently stuff the body and sew shut the bottom. Add eyes, mouth, and other features with buttons, thread, or fabric pieces. (You can also do this before you sew the big circles together.)

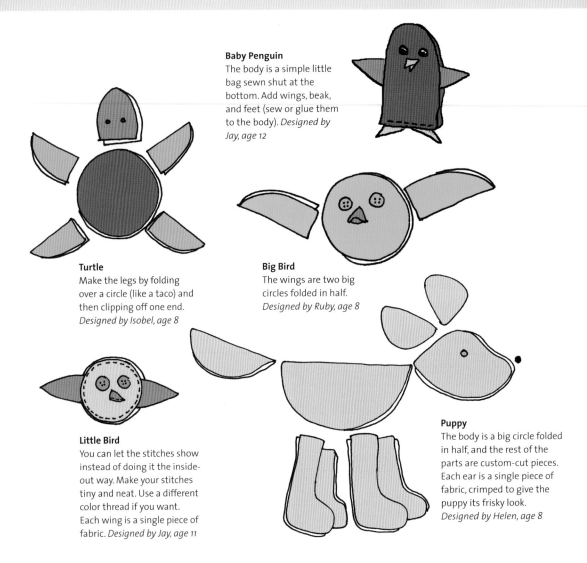

Baby Penguin
The body is a simple little bag sewn shut at the bottom. Add wings, beak, and feet (sew or glue them to the body). *Designed by Jay, age 12*

Turtle
Make the legs by folding over a circle (like a taco) and then clipping off one end. *Designed by Isobel, age 8*

Big Bird
The wings are two big circles folded in half. *Designed by Ruby, age 8*

Little Bird
You can let the stitches show instead of doing it the inside-out way. Make your stitches tiny and neat. Use a different color thread if you want. Each wing is a single piece of fabric. *Designed by Jay, age 11*

Puppy
The body is a big circle folded in half, and the rest of the parts are custom-cut pieces. Each ear is a single piece of fabric, crimped to give the puppy its frisky look. *Designed by Helen, age 8*

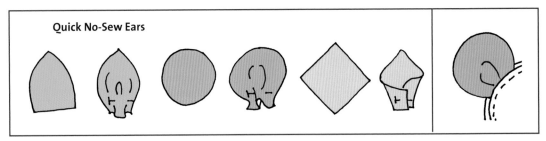

Quick No-Sew Ears

Kite

Project designed by Ezri Tarazi

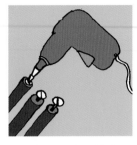

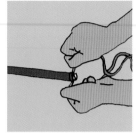

1. Cut four sticks of light wood or bamboo to the same length (around 48 inches). Drill a small hole at both ends of each stick and insert screws into the holes.

2. Drill a hole in the middle of every stick. Connect all of the sticks in the middle with a screw.

3. Tie a long string to a screw at the end of one of the sticks. Pull the long end of the string to the middle of the stick and mark the distance on the string.

4. Take the string to the end of the next stick and tie it where you marked it. Repeat to the next stick until you get the form of a hexagon. All the strings around should be tight.

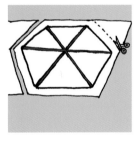

5. Place a plastic sheet under the hexagon, and cut the sheet a bit larger than the hexagon. You can decorate the sheet with markers on either or both sides.

6. Make a small cut in the sheet at every corner. Fold the sheet over the strings and tape the edges with heavy packing tape.

HELP!
This is a big project. Kids will need help with tools.

7. Turn the kite upside down. Use the adhesive tape and pieces of colored ribbon to make the kite's "hair." Tape the ribbons to each side of the hexagon.

8. Cut three pieces of string that are each a little bit longer than the length of a rib. Tie the three pieces together at one end, and tie each one to the kite at the other end—one in the center and two at adjacent stick ends—so they will form together a pyramid.

?! ?! ?! ⊕⊕⊕ ✹✹✹ ⓢⓢ

9. Cut two more pieces of rope the length of a rib. Connect them to the bottom of the kite to form a triangle. Now, tear old shirts or other clothing into long strips. Tie the strips together into a long string and connect them to the bottom of the triangle. You'll have to do some testing when you fly the kite. If the tail is not long enough the kite will not be stable. If it's too long and heavy, the wind will not lift the kite up into the air.

10. Finally, connect a very long piece of string to the end of the pyramid. This is the string you will use to fly the kite.

Now the kite is ready to fly. You'll need to make sure that it's windy enough before you try flying the kite. Ask a friend to come with you. One of you holds the kite with two hands, vertically to the ground. The other holds the rope and stretches it thirty feet or so from the kite. Adjust your kite to the right position against the wind, and then throw it up, allowing the wind to lift it into the air.

Box Buildings

Build a house, a city, a hotel, or a hospital out of boxes. Use old boxes, or make your own. Create cars and furniture out of bottle caps, fabric, foam, and other stuff you find around the house.

TRY IT!
Cut holes or flaps for windows and doors.

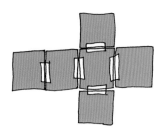

Basic Box Building

1. Cut six squares of paper, cardboard, or card stock. Lay out the squares in a crossroad pattern. Tape together.

2. Fold the taped squares into a cube. Tape shut.

Second-Grade City
Kids in a second-grade class laid out a town plan with square sheets of paper (green for grass, black for streets). Then they added box buildings (houses, school, police/fire station, mall), leaving lots of room for ponds and playgrounds. *Special thanks to Marilyn Milton, The Park School, Baltimore.*

Hotel Origami
Designed by Ruby, age 7

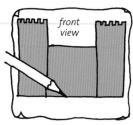

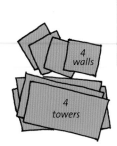

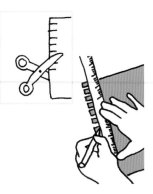

1. Find a piece of flat cardboard to use as a base. (Ours is 16 inches square.) Make a drawing of the ground view (plan) of your castle. Draw towers, walls, etc.

2. Make another drawing of the front view of the castle (elevation), showing how tall the towers and walls will be.

3. Cut out a piece of cardboard for each tower and wall. Our tower pieces are 10 inches wide by 8 inches tall; walls are 5 inches square.

4. To create a castle edge (crenellation), make short cuts with scissors; then use an X-acto knife and ruler to cut through every other tab. Ask an adult for help.

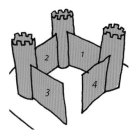

5. Roll the tower pieces and tape them shut with heavy packing tape. (Scotch tape or masking tape isn't strong enough.) Attach the first tower to the base with hot glue.

6. Glue a wall to the tower and the base, and then glue the second tower to the wall and the base.

7. Continue working around the castle: wall, tower, wall.

8. Attach the last wall to the first tower *before* installing the final tower. This makes the building connect better.

OUCH
Careful with the glue gun! Never touch the tip or let hot glue drip on you.

TIPS • Cereal boxes are great for this project. You can cut them easily with scissors, and they roll up well for making the towers. Take apart the box at the seams and flatten it out. • To cut out a bunch of pieces the same size, measure the first piece, and then trace around it.

Corn Flake Castle

This plain-vanilla castle has a simple square floorplan. Create variations with odd-shaped layouts, square turrets, drawbridges, outer walls, and more. (See the fancy buildings on the following pages for more ideas.) *Designed by Jay, age 11*

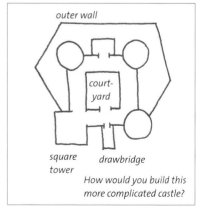

outer wall

court-yard

square tower

drawbridge

How would you build this more complicated castle?

Project designed by Marla Hollandsworth, The Park School, Baltimore

Made for a fifth-grade class project, these models were built the same way as our castle on pages 82–83. The models are based on photographs and drawings of real historic buildings. Made with corrugated cardboard and then painted, they took five weeks to build!

Hagia Sofia, Turkey
Built as a Byzantine church in 537 AD, Hagia Sofia later became a mosque. The domes in the model are made from Styrofoam spheres from a craft store. The pale green is like the color of a copper roof. *Designed by Yen, age 11*

Krak des Chevaliers, Syria
This castle was occuppied by warriors during the Crusades. *Designed by Ben, age 11*

Angkor Wat, Cambodia
This temple, built in 1113 AD, is one of the world's largest religious buildings. *Designed by Jay, age 11*

?! ?! ?! ⏰⏰⏰ 💥 💥 💥 💲 💲

Product designers make useful objects, from cars and bikes to clocks and coffee pots. They use materials, colors, and shapes to help make things easy to use and fun to look at. Inna Alesina works in Baltimore, Maryland. She designs shoes, backpacks, sports equipment, and furniture. Can you guess why the pin cushion she designed doesn't pop when you stick pins in it?*

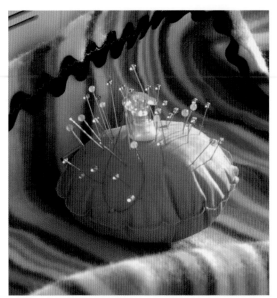

When did you decide to become a designer?
I grew up in the Ukraine, a country in Eastern Europe. I began studying fine art in college, and then I found out about product design. I like making things that are useful.

What did you make when you were a kid?
I made my own clothes by sewing, dying, knitting, and repurposing old clothes. I also liked macramé, beading, and making things to wear, to decorate my house, and to give as gifts.

What is your dream project?
I would like to design something I haven't designed before: a baby stroller, a toothbrush, a tent, or even a mailbox. I like projects that might make someone's life more fun, safe, or productive.

* The pool-toy valve and the shiny material make the pin cushion look like it's full of air, but actually, it has pillow stuffing inside.

HOME

Graffiti Furniture

Putting graffiti on your walls (or anyone else's) is a bad idea, unless somebody invites you to do it. But writing and drawing on cheap or recycled furniture can be lots of fun. (You'll still need your parents to tell you what's okay to scribble on.)

Graffiti Couch
This low-cost couch from IKEA makes a great surface for Sharpie drawings.

Photos: Jason Knauer

PARTY ON!
Invite your friends to help.

Savage Side Table

This thrift-shop side table had ugly scratches and water stains on it. Now it's covered with artwork, too.

Designed by Ruby and Jay, ages 5 and 9

Arty Art Table

Instead of worrying about getting markers on your table, why not find a work table that you can draw on? Ask your parents to buy a cheap white table, or paint an old one with gesso.

Decorated Boxes

Boxes are useful for storing your stuff or for packing up gifts. So many boxes get thrown away each day, especially around the holidays. Why not make them beautiful and unique by adding your own designs?

SAVE IT! Bring old boxes back to life.

Decoupage Boxes

1. Cut cereal boxes into sizes and shapes you like, or find an old gift box or other container.

2. Cover with paper using a glue stick or library paste.

3. Paint them with decoupage glue (Mod Podge is good) for extra shine and durability.

4. When your boxes are dry, add colored tape, buttons, beads, or tiny toys to make them even more spectacular.

Supply Boxes
These boxes are covered with our own patterned paper. The patterns were made by scanning ordinary objects—coins, ribbons, rubber bands, and wooden letters. (For instructions, see page 30.) What perfect boxes for stashing money and supplies! We added some abandoned Barbie shoes and other old plastic toys to give our boxes an extra hit of fun. *Designed by Isabel, Eliot, Hannah, and Danielle, ages 6–9*

GIVE IT!
Decorated
boxes make
great gifts.

Store your zines, draw-
ings, notebooks, and
other stuff in a box
decorated with your
own designs. These are
made from inexpensive
magazine boxes from
IKEA. Cover the boxes
with patterned paper
and glue other pictures
on top. Add tape, ribbons,
and anything else you
like for a cool and crazy
look.

Monogram Madness

After we covered the boxes
with pretty paper, we added
our names using fancy clip-
art initials. The black-and-
white graphics stand out
against the colored paper
background. *Designed by
Eliot, Hannah, and Ronnie,
ages 6–9*

Flik Box

This box features kids'
drawings. *Designed by
Orr, age 9*

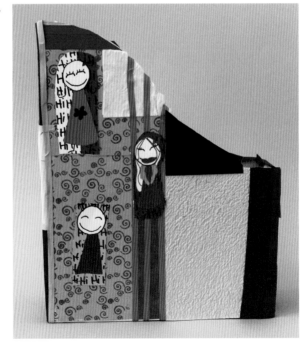

Friendship Chest
The black paper borders around the photos make them stand out against the patterned background.
Designed by Lucy, age 6

This decorated box is great for storing pencils, jewelry, photos, or cards.

1. Find a box with a hinged lid. Cover it with a first layer of paper. Trace the sides of the box. Cut out pieces of paper to match each side. Use wrapping paper, scraps of collage paper, or a pattern you draw yourself.

2. Put glue stick all over the back of each piece of paper and press down firmly onto box.

3. Cut out your photos and lay them out on the top of the box. Arrange some pictures on the sides of the box, too.

4. Glue the photos onto the box. If you want, coat the box with decoupage medium or shellac. Test the coating first to make sure the photos won't smudge and smear.

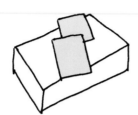

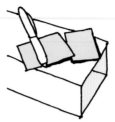

1. Cut out your photos, cropping (cutting off) parts you don't want.

2. Take a big cereal box and cut off the top flaps. Lay out photos on one side of the box. They should flow from the top of the box to the middle. Make a regular stepping pattern or a crazier set of diagonals.

3. Trace along the top edge of your photos. The photos can overlap each other, and they can wrap around the sides of the box.

4. Following the line you've traced, cut away this part of the box as well as the top part of the narrow front.

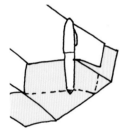

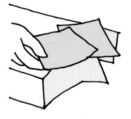

5. Lay the box on its side. Using the new line that you've cut, retrace the same line onto the inside of the other side of the box. Cut out the other side. (You'll want to have a similar set of photos to lay out on the other side.)

6. Cover your box with paper. Use wrapping paper, sheets of scrap paper, or a pattern that you make yourself. Rub glue stick across the entire back surface of your paper. Press down firmly. You can use the long edge of a popsicle stick to smooth out air bubbles and extra glue.

7. Now, glue on your photos. You may want to put them on top of a piece of colored paper first as a frame, and then attach the combination to your box.

8. The narrow front of the box is the "spine" of your container, showing its face to the world. You can put your name here, or the date of the photos you're storing, or the name of the project ("friendship file").

Designed by Hannah, age 9

?!?! ⊕⊕⊕ ❧ ❧ ❧ ⑨⑨

Magnets

Magnets are fun and functional. Use them to post lists, phone numbers, or your favorite art. They can also be works of art in their own right. Magnets make great gifts, favors, and party activities.

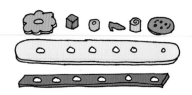

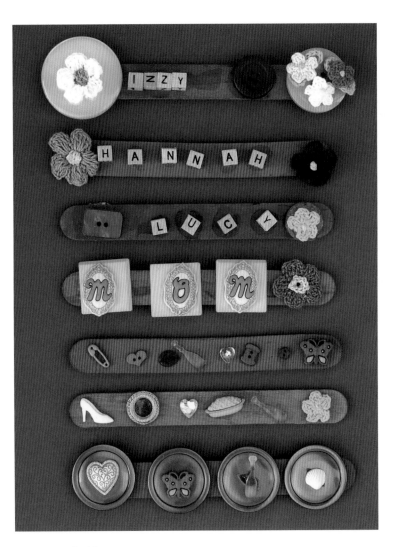

Popsicle Stick Magnets

1. Glue beads, buttons, google eyes, puff balls, or other small objects to a popsicle stick.

2. When it's dry, stick on or glue magnet strips to back of popsicle stick. (Your stick may be heavy, so use plenty of magnetic material, which you can buy at an office supply store.)

3. The long shape is handy for your name or an important phone number.

Magnetic Museum

Tiny drawings make great magnets. Stick a small drawing directly to a magnet, or scan a big drawing, reduce the size, print it, cut it out, and then apply to a magnet.

Magnet projects designed by Lucy, Isabel, Ruby, and Hannah, ages 6–9

Word Game

Make your own magnetic word game in Word or another computer program.

1. Open up a new document and choose a plain typeface such as Helvetica or Arial. Make your letters bold, and make them size 14. Draw a line at the top of the page by typing a lot of hyphens and hitting the return button..

2. Skip a line and type some funny or interesting nouns (people, places, or things). Put three spaces after every word, to leave room for cutting. When you fill up a line, skip another line and use hyphens to draw another line.

3. Create a few rows of verbs and describing word (adjectives and adverbs). Add some connecting words such as *to, from*, and *but*. You will also need some short words like *the, her, his*, and *it*.

4. When you have enough words, stick your page onto a sheet of magnetic paper. You can also cut your paper into smaller pieces and stick them onto business card magnets.

5. Cut the magnet along the lines and then snip the words apart.

6. Put the words together to make funny sentences.

Fashion Magnets

Make a mix-and-match fashion collection with sticky-back business card magnets.

1. On a sheet of paper, trace a magnet six times (two rows with three magnets each).

2. Draw a line half-way through the first row of magnets. You will now have squares for six little magnets and three big magnets.

3. Draw purses in the top row. Draw shirts in the middle row. Draw skirts and pants in the bottom row.

4. Cut out your drawings and stick them on magnets. (Two little drawings will fit on one magnet.) Mix and match!

Magnets designed by Ruby, age 7

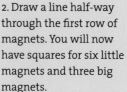

TIPS • You can recycle magnet cards from the dentist's office or the pizza joint. • Or, print images onto sheets of magnetic paper.

Party Supplies

The party aisle at your local megastore is filled with prefab cups, napkins, and goody bags. Why not make your own personalized decorations with inexpensive picnic ware or plates and silverware borrowed from the china cabinet?

Party Picnic Goods

1. Draw a cool character. Scan or photocopy your character and print it out in different sizes.

2. Stick your character on paper cups, goody bags, and flatware wrapped in a strip of paper.

3. For a quick and easy placemat, tape together two sheets of paper.

MORE IDEAS
Put your character on your own custom party favors. Send your friends home with a pack of stickers, a tin of mints, or a T-shirt, all imprinted with your awesome character.

Party Animal
The one-eyed bunny is *everywhere* at this casual birthday party.

The funky setup uses cheap picnic stuff. *Character designed by Jay, age 11*

Paper Napkin Rings

A fun and easy way to set a festive table is to wrap your napkins and flatware with a paper band. Use wrapping paper, scrapbook paper, or comic books. This design doubles as a place card. (See more place card ideas on the following page.)

SAVE IT!
Combine paper scraps with real china, silverware, and fabrics.

Paper and Cloth
We used paper decorations to customize some napkins from the linen drawer.
Designed by Ruby, age 7

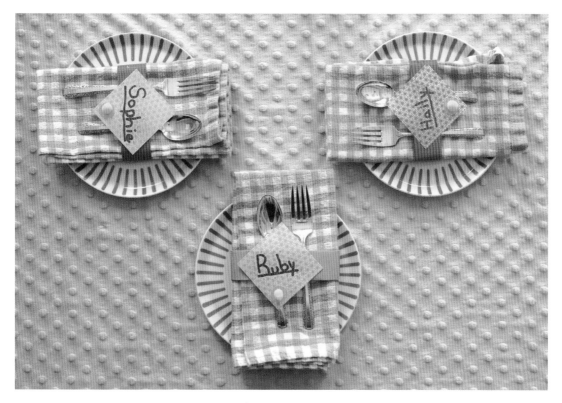

Make place cards for your next party, whether it's tea for your stuffed animals or a fancy formal event. A place card goes at everyone's plate, letting each guest know where to sit. People and stuffies alike enjoy knowing that the hostess has a plan.

Rubber Stamp Place Cards
Stamp each card with a guest's initials.

Illustrate the cards with a surprise drawing.

Designed by Ruby, age 7

Fancy Paper Place Card
Fold a small piece of fancy paper in half. Add a white sticker on top. Write your guest's name on the sticker.

Designed by Ronnie, age 9

Pop-Up Place Cards

1. Design a square card with a picture that extends across the two halves of the card. Draw each card by hand, or print or photocopy them.

2. Cut out each card. Using an X-Acto knife, cut around the part of the card that will pop up.

3. Gently fold the card, leaving the pop-up part unfolded.

Cockatoo Card
The child's painting on the front of the card is partly cut out so that it pops up. The fantasy map on the back of the card was watercolored and then scanned. The full map is copied onto the reverse side of the card so that the flipped-up interior is pretty, too. These cards were for a formal bat mitzvah party. *Painting by Ilana, age 10*

Theme Parties

Holidays like Halloween and Valentine's Day are great excuses to throw a party. Instead of buying decorations at the mall, have fun (and save some money) making your own.

Tween Halloween Party
These funky party goods set the tone for a chilling funfest with your friends.

Ghoulish Goody Bags
The simple drawings are cut out and glued on paper bags.
Designed by Lucy and Isabel, age 6

Spook Mark
Skinny vampires make great book marks (and an easy party favor).

Spooky Invitation
We did the drawing on old-school construction paper and scanned the results. Party info was added in Photoshop.

Spooky CD
To design a label for your own spooky CD, make your artwork the same size as the insert that comes with the blank CD.

Spooky Candy
Wrap candy bars in your own graphics. (Keep the original wrapper underneath in case your friends have allergies.)

Drawings by Hannah and Ronnie, age 9.

Imagine a party where every–thing is fluffy: the decorations, the activities, the food, even the guests. To create our fluffy party, we made soft and cozy decorations out of fleece and other materials.

Fluffy Goody Bags

We bought plain bags and glued on animal heads cut from scraps of fluffy fleece. You could also use paper, felt, or other fabric.

Designed by Ruby, age 7

> **MORE IDEAS** What other words could become a party theme? Try blue, green, crazy, alien, slimy, lacy, loud, fruity, fancy, furry, or striped.

Fluffy Cup Cozies

These cups are wrapped in fuzzy jackets. Make them yourself, or ask your friends to help for a fun party activity.
Designed by Ruby, age 7

Fluffy Cup Cozies

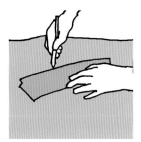

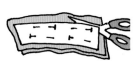

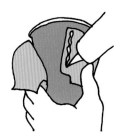

1. Get a cardboard cup wrapper from a coffee shop.

2. Take it apart at the seam and stretch it out flat. Trace around the cup wrapper onto a piece of paper to make a pattern. Cut out the pattern.

3. Pin the pattern to your fabric. (If you are making a bunch of cozies for a party, pin and cut through two layers of fabric at once to save time.)

4. Wrap the fabric tightly around a paper cup, and apply hot glue along the "tab" edge of the fabric. Firmly press down the other fabric edge over the glue. This is tricky, so ask a grownup to help.

OUCH!
Careful with
the hot glue!

Kitty

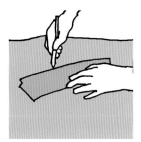

Bear

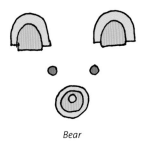

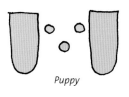

Puppy

5. Now, for the fun part! Cut out eyes, ears, mouths, and other features. You can also use buttons, puff balls, and ribbons.

Make bunnies, kitties, aliens, and more. Hot-glue them to the cup cozy.

TIPS • You can also do this project with colored paper instead of fabric. • The cozies look best on plain-colored cups. If you can't find ones you like, wrap colored paper around a printed paper cup. (Make a pattern by cutting one cup open along the seam and laying it out flat.)

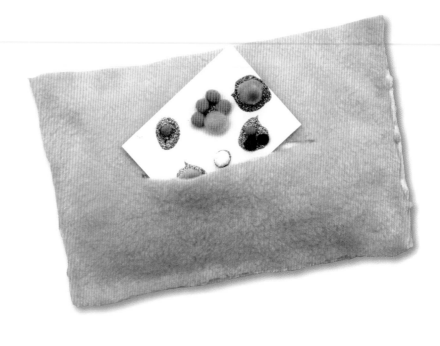

DO ME A FAVOR!
Let your guests make their own party favors.

Fluffy Pencil

Get some pencils with add-on erasers. Tuck a circle of netting or thin fabric under the eraser. Make a crazy finger grip with fleece, ribbons, and pom-poms.

Designed by Nathalie, age 8

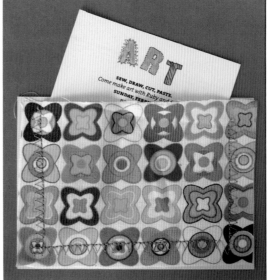

More Fabric Invitations: Stitched Envelope

Using a plain index card as a pattern, cut out a scrap of fabric. On a sewing machine, stitch the fabric to the card, leaving one side open to make an envelope. If you don't have a sewing machine, glue the fabric instead, or sew it by hand. Tuck a note inside.

Designed by Ruby, age 8

Fluffy Invitation

1. Cut out a piece of paper the size you want your invitation to be. Using the paper as a pattern, cut out one piece of cardboard and two pieces of fleece for each invitation.

2. Put hot glue around the edge of the card-board, leaving one edge open. Attach one piece of the fleece.

3. Put a little stuffing inside the fleece pocket. (Don't use too much, or the cardboard will start to bend.)

4. Glue down the open edge and press firmly.

OUCH!
Careful with the hot glue!

  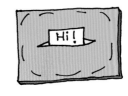 

5. Fold the second layer of fleece in half. Cut a slit starting at the fold.

6. Glue the top layer onto your little pillow, sealing up all four sides.

7. Create an invitation to slip inside the pillow slot. It can be a flat card or a folded sheet.

8. Let the top of the invitation peek out of the pillow.

TIPS • Address the invitation on the flat cardboard side. • If you're mailing it, put it inside a real "padded envelope" from an office supply store. • We used fleece for this project because it's fluffy and it doesn't come apart at the edges. Felt works well for the same reasons.

Fashion designers create patterns and prototypes for clothing. Couture designers make one-of-a-kind pieces. Claire Joseph runs a small store in Los Angeles stocked with clothing she designs and sews herself, often using fabric that she dyes in her kitchen studio. She also designs custom gowns and other dresses for special clients.

When did you decide to become a designer?

My mother taught me that an artist creates solely for personal expression, while a designer fulfills the needs of others. I didn't think I had a clear enough vision to be a fine artist, but I was smart enough to go out and get a job. My grandmother taught me to sew as a child, so I was able to work in the fashion business.

What did you make when you were a kid?

I liked dripping nail polish onto Plexiglas, embroidering burlap tapestries, and sewing stuff. I also helped my mother with her architecture and sculpture work.

What is your dream project?

After seven years of making couture clothing, I am interested in designing fabric that could be produced industrially in small runs.

FASHION

Fashion Sketching

Fashion designers don't invent every new outfit from scratch. Many designs are put together out of basic sleeves, skirts, necklines, and other parts. Just as you put together a great outfit with clothes from your own closet, fashion designers get ideas by looking at what's already out there. Sketching with pencil on paper, they put the parts together in their own ways and add the fabrics, colors, details, and trimmings.

zipper front

petal neck

Use our fashion design chart to invent some cool outfits. Combine a sharp neckline with interesting sleeves; tie it all together with a flouncy or narrow skirt.

Our chart includes some of the classics that the professionals use, but we couldn't resist putting in a few silly ideas. Hint: the turtle neck is real, but some of the other animals aren't. Invent some new classics of your own.

boat neck

turtle neck

button collar

poodle neck

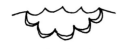

scalloped neck

doggy cone

halter top

bottle neck

square neck

sweetheart neck

ruff neck

V neck

lion neck

keyhole neck

?! ⊕ 🐛 ⊕

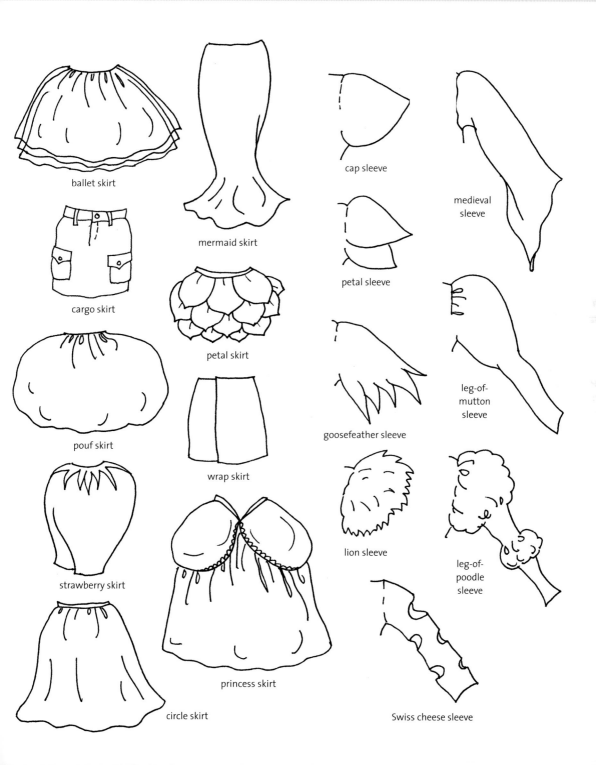

ballet skirt

mermaid skirt

cap sleeve

medieval sleeve

cargo skirt

petal sleeve

petal skirt

goosefeather sleeve

leg-of-mutton sleeve

pouf skirt

wrap skirt

strawberry skirt

lion sleeve

leg-of-poodle sleeve

princess skirt

circle skirt

Swiss cheese sleeve

poodle coat

ballet skirt with
single-sleeve top

bottle-neck sweater with
Swiss cheese sleeves

Fashion Sketching
Kids made these
fashion designs inspired
by our chart on the
previous page. Have fun
mixing and matching
elements and inventing
your own. Create
fabulous accessories
and intriguing color
combinations. Try
cutting dresses out of
patterned paper, too.

chocolate-striped, angle-cut
sleeveless dress

cargo skirt with
polka dot halter top

poodle-sleeve
prom dress

*Drawings by Ruby
and Isabella, ages 7–8*

mermaid dresses

goosefeather dress

poodle-neck, poodle-sleeve,
puff-bottom dress

petal-sleeve
layer dress

billiard skirt

ruffled skirts

Sketching on the computer lets you make different versions of the same design. Use the "Layer" feature in Photoshop to experiment with colors and patterns.

NERD ALERT! This project requires some basic Photoshop knowledge.

1. Open a new file in Photoshop. Make the file 500 x 500 pixels, 300 pixels per inch. Make it transparent.

With the pencil tool, draw an outline of a skirt. (Leave room for a shirt above it.)

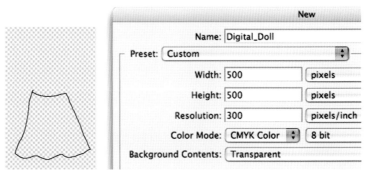

2. Open the "Layers" palette (Window>Layers). Now, click on the layer icon on the bottom of the Layers window to add a new layer. Draw a shirt in your new layer. Each layer is like a sheet of paper. You can draw or color on one sheet at a time (just click on the layer you want to work on). Click on the eye icon to make the layer disappear.

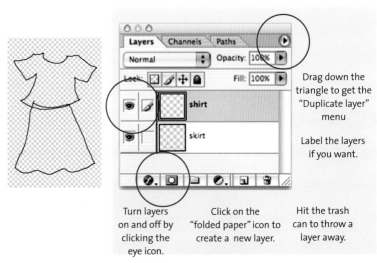

Drag down the triangle to get the "Duplicate layer" menu

Label the layers if you want.

Turn layers on and off by clicking the eye icon.

Click on the "folded paper" icon to create a new layer.

Hit the trash can to throw a layer away.

3. Now, make copies of your shirt layer and your skirt layer.

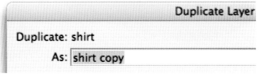

4. Use the paint bucket, the pencil, and even the eraser to change each of the copies of your shirt and skirt, making new outfits.

The layers can interact with each other. Here, the green layer is on top of the red layer. We used the eraser tool to "cut holes" in the green layer, so that you can see the red dots underneath!

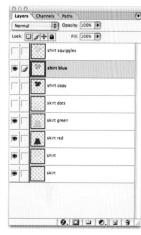

5. The yellow shirt is on top of the blue shirt. We used the eraser tool to erase lines in the yellow layer, showing the blue layer underneath.

The purple dots and x's are drawn on a layer that is on top of the green layer.

You can change the order of the layers by dragging them up and down in the stack. Make layers turn on and off by clicking the eye icon.

TIP Make sure your shirt and skirt outlines are completely closed (no gaps). Otherwise, the bucket will fill up the whole layer, not just your drawing.

Graffiti Accessories

Graffiti Shoes

Sketch on your shoes with permanent marker. (Ask your parents first.) Draw characters, decorations, stick figures, or names. Cheap canvas shoes work fine, but leather (or fake leather) shoes allow you to make the best line.

Designed by Ruby, Jay, and Jean-Claude, ages 7–11

Graffiti Bags

For a fun party souvenir, give each guest a cotton bag. After writing your name on your bag, pass your bag to the left. Write a quick note to the girl whose bag you have, then pass on to the next guest. Everyone leaves with a chain letter from her party friends.

Designed by Ruby, Isobel, Helen, Nathalie, Sarah, and Isa, ages 7–8

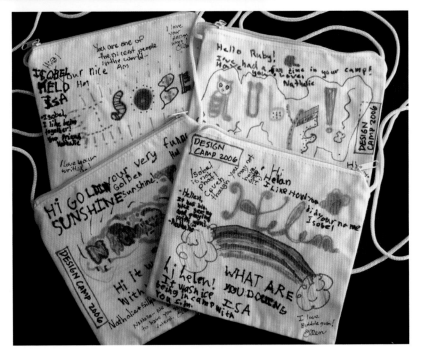

Graffiti Wrist Bands

On a wrist band that you make or buy, draw initials and secret symbols to represent all your friends. Make letters out of dots and squiggles. Make hieroglyphs (Egyptian letters) that look like eyes, snakes, or birds. We used only three colors (red, black, and silver), so the bracelets all look good together.

Designed by Helen, Nathalie, Ruby, Isa, Isobel, and Sarah, ages 7–8

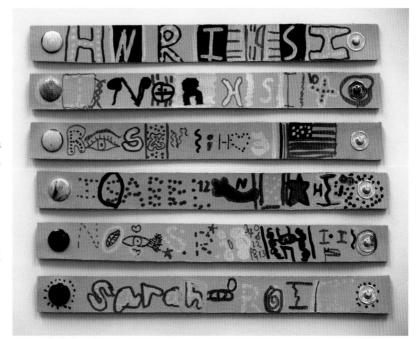

Ribbon Accessories

Use ribbons to customize plain purses and wristbands. Mix, match, and overlap to create exciting combinations. Save all your scraps, because every little bit counts. (It doesn't take much ribbon to make an awesome ring.)

1. Get a bag or wrist band to decorate, or make your own bag or wrist band with paper or fabric. Gather up some scraps of ribbon and fabric.

2. Arrange layers and stripes in interesting combinations until you find a combination that you love.

3. Use hot glue or fabric glue to hold it all together.

Tiny Ribbon Purse
This itty bitty purse is made from two scraps of ribbon glued together. *Designed by Ruby, age 8*

Designed by Helen, Isabella,
Ruby, and Marley, ages 7–9

Decoupage Purses

Spiff up an old vinyl handbag or a toy purse you've outgrown by covering it with scraps of paper and fabric. This technique is called "decoupage," from the French word meaning "to cut up."

RECYCLE!
With a little effort, even your Mom's old stuff can be cool again.

1. Find an old purse with a smooth surface—vinyl or leather. Rub the surface of the purse with sandpaper.

2. Cover the outside of the purse with gesso (a white acrylic base paint available at art stores). Do one side at a time, letting each one dry.

3. Leave white, or add a coat of colored acrylic paint. When the purse is dry, put a generous layer of Mod Podge or another decoupage glue on the surface of the purse.

4. Add paper or fabric elements, and then put more glue medium on top. The extra glue helps your pieces stick to the purse, and also makes it more-or-less waterproof.

Designed by Hannah, Isabel, Lucy, and Eliot, ages 6–9

Customized T-Shirts

Why wear someone else's brand when you can design your own? Draw directly on T-shirts using fabric paints, pens, or ink sticks, or reproduce any kind of drawing, photo, or graphic using iron-on transfers. Use clever cutting and sewing to change the shape and style of the shirt itself.

OUCH!
Irons sure are hot. Get help from an adult with ironing.

Transfer Shirts

1. Draw or scan a graphic, or make a design using Photoshop, Word, or another software program.

2. Iron-on transfer paper is available at office supply stores. Print your graphic following the instructions in the package. You will probably have to "flip" your image.

3. Place the printed graphic on your shirt, and iron it on, following the instructions from the package. Some products have to cool before you peel off the backing paper.

4. Look for instructions for how to wash your shirt. You may be asked to wash it in cold water the first time so that colors don't bleed.

Designed Jay, Eliot, Miriam, Ruby, and Ronnie, ages 6–11

For a party, make a bunch of shirts ahead of time using iron-on transfer graphics. Then go wild with the decorations! Apply fabric paints with a brush—or splatter it on straight from the jar.

Skeleton and Clown Shirts
Designed by Lucy, Orr, and Ronnie, ages 6–10. Clip art from *Skeletons*, published by Pepin Press (www.pepinpress.com).

Dye sticks and fabric crayons
(available at craft stores) make
fuzzy lines, not crisp ones.
Try covering the entire surface
of your shirt with a single word,
or pile on layers of marks and
scratches. Heat-set with an iron
before washing. You can also
draw directly on a T-shirt with a
fabric marker.

Scrawl Shirts
Designed by Hannah, age 9

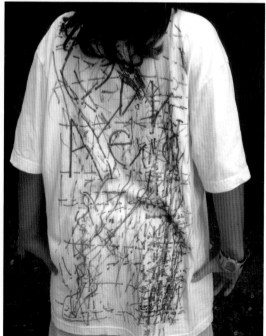

Appliqué is a decorative sewing technique in which one layer of fabric is stitched onto another. In "reverse appliqué," you sew a piece of fabric *underneath* the main fabric instead of sewing on top of it. Then you cut a window into the top layer to reveal the piece underneath. This project uses simple squares or rectangles of fabric, but if you are patient, you can make fancier designs like flowers, leaves, or animals.

1. Cut out a square of interesting fabric that looks good with the shirt you want to decorate. (You can also decorate a pillow, bag, or jacket.) Use one piece of fabric, or make a design with several pieces.

2. Turn the shirt inside out and place the fabric piece "right" side down. Pin it into place, being careful to go through just one layer of the T-shirt.

3. Sew around the piece of fabric. A simple straight shape like a square is easy to sew on a sewing machine. A curvy shape is easier to sew by hand.

4. Turn the shirt right-side out. Carefully snip away a window into the shirt, cutting neatly alongside your stitches. Make sure you don't cut into the fabric underneath.

5. When you have finished cutting, you will see the new layer of fabric underneath.

6. You can leave the edge the way it is, or finish it off with a fancy stitch like a zig zag, sewing from the "right side" of the T-shirt. Add pieces to the front and back of the shirt until you like your design.

?! ?! ?! ⊕⊕ ⊕ 🐾 🐾 ⓘ⓪

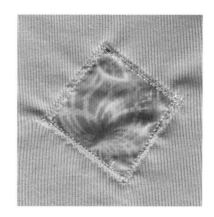

Designed by Helen and Graysen, age 8

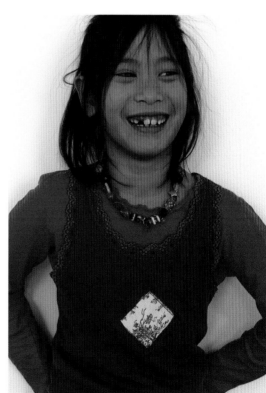

Stencil Shirts

Use stencils and spray paint to put graphics on T-shirts, hoodies, denim jackets, and more. Make your own stencils, recycle stuff from your art supply bin, or buy stencils from a hardware or craft store. Stenciled spray paint makes an interesting effect. Some edges will be soft and fuzzy, while others will be crisp and hard, depending on how flat the stencil is lying on the surface.

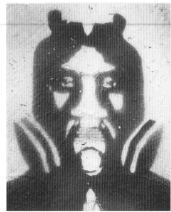

Make your own stencils
Make a simple drawing on card stock. Cut out the parts that you want to paint with an X-Acto knife. All the parts of the drawing have to stay attached, or they will "fall out" when you pick up the stencil.

Designed by Tycho, age 13

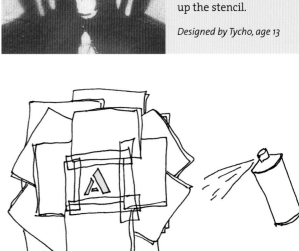

1. Find a place outdoors to work, and lay down a lot of newspaper on the ground.

2. Lay down the garment you want to paint on the paper. Smooth it out so that it's as flat as possible.

3. Attach the stencil to your garment with heavy clear packing tape. Cover all the edges of the stencil, so that paint can't get in under the tape.

4. Tape another layer of newspaper on top of the stencil, covering all the parts of the garment except the parts you want to paint. Use a lot of paper; spray paint will creep in under any open flaps or edges!

5. Spray! Keep your hand moving, so you don't get heavy, shiny parts.

THIS STINKS!
Work outside and wear a mask when working with spray paint.

Helvetica Girl
Writing out words with spray paint and stencils can be tricky, but it's easy to print all the letters at once. *Designed by Isabella, age 8*

Sweet Street Stuff
A plastic paper-doll template gets an urban update in this spray-painted T-shirt. *Designed by Ruby, age 8*

Fringe/Tube Shirt

This shirt is made of two pieces: a tube top and a fringed overlayer. You can make both pieces from T-shirts, or use a tube top you already have.

To make the overlayer:

1. Cut off a large T-shirt beneath the sleeves. Cut at one seam to make a big rectangle. Turn the rectangle upside down so that the hemmed part is at the top. Cut the fabric into long fringes, leaving 2–3 inches at the top.

2. Measure so that the length of the fringed rectangle matches the circumference of your tube top, leaving an inch for a seam, then sew the top band together so that it makes a tube.

3. Fit the fringed tube over a chair back or someone's body, and begin tying the fringes. First row: tie pairs of fringes together, about two inches down, all around.

4. Second row: again, tie pairs together, but now your ties will connect together the pairs you made on the first row. Continue until you have as many rows as you like.

5. Put the fringed layer on top of the tube top and pin them together around the top edge. Sew together.

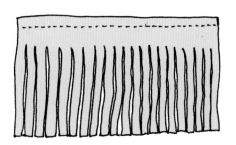

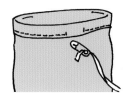

To make a tube top:

1. Cut a T-shirt below the sleeves. Use the hemmed part of the T-shirt as the bottom of your tube top.

2. Cut one side seam to form a rectangle. Wrap the rectangle around your chest, with the "right" side of the fabric against your body. Pull it close to your chest so that it fits snugly. Pin the seam. Cut off extra fabric. Sew the seam by hand or with a sewing machine.

3. Cut a piece of elastic that fits snugly around your chest above your bust line, plus a few extra inches. Fold top of rectangle down to form a pocket wider than your elastic. Sew to form a narrow tube across the top of your rectangle. Leave an opening where you can insert the elastic.

4. Stick a safety pin through the elastic and push it through the pocket. Make sure you don't pull the end of the elastic all the way through, or you will have to start over! Sew the two ends of the elastic together firmly, by hand or on the sewing machine.

5. Add straps to the tube top if you like.

Laced-Up Shirt

1. Cut a T-shirt up the side seams, all the way through the arm holes.

2. Pin the two seams back together.

3. Use the tip of a sharp pair of scissors to punch holes through both layers of the shirt, on both sides.

4. Restitch the sides by lacing a long piece of ribbon or string, or a long strip from a T-shirt, through the holes. Start at the top, tie at the bottom, and leave some hanging at the bottom.

  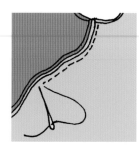 

1. Choose two shirts the same size. Carefully cut the collars off the shirts, and cut each shirt in half. Do the cutting on a flat surface.

2. Take opposite halves from each shirt (one left and one right), and turn them inside out. Pin together carefully.

3. Stitch up both sides, by hand or on a sewing machine.

4. Sleeve detail: you can cut off the sleeves and tie them up with contrasting ribbons made out of scraps from the sleeves.

Variation: Half Pint
Cut two shirts in half horizontally, then pin and sew the two tubes together. Try it with three tubes, too, or as many as you like.

Variation: The Zag
Cut first shirt on a diagonal, somewhere below the arm hole. Use the scrap as a pattern to cut off bottom of the second shirt. Pin and sew.

MORE IDEAS These shirts were inspired by Megan Nicolay's book *Generation T* (Workman, 2006). See her book for more amazing projects!

?! ?! ?! ☺☺☺ ✴✴✴ ∅$

Fleece Scarves

Project designed by Lynn Mally

Wrap yourself up in a warm, fuzzy scarf, made with your own personal style. Fleece comes in bright colors and simple prints. When you cut it, fleece doesn't fray, so you don't have to hem it. It's a great fabric for kids learning to sew.

NICE STUFF!
Fleece is made from recycled soda bottles.

Lay out a length of fleece (2 yards), and cut a long, straight strip (1 foot).

Or, cut two narrower strips in different colors (6 inches each), and sew together.

Or, cut rectangles of color, and sew them together.

Decorative Add-Ons
Cut out skinny strips of fleece in different colors, and add soft, fuzzy ribbon designs. Make flowers by folding and winding strips of fleece. Sew decorations to scarf.

Designed by Lucy, age 6

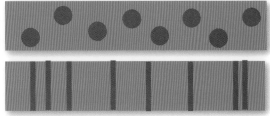

To add polka dots or skinnier stripes, cut out shapes from fleece. Use fabric glue to attach pieces of fleece to your scarf. (Use lots of glue, as the fleece is very absorbent.) You can also sew your patterns on. To make our polka dot scarf, we glued on the dots and then added stitches on the sewing machine for extra strength.

MORE IDEAS • Make pockets by folding up the ends and sewing on both sides. • Make fringes by cutting skinny strips at the ends. • Make a warmer scarf by sewing together two long pieces of fleece on three sides (like a long bag), then turn the bag right-side-out to hide the seams; sew shut.

?! ?! ⊕ ⊕ ⊕ 🐾 🐾 🐾 ⓓ ⓓ

Big Bold Scarves
Designed by Hannah and Orr,
age 9

Aprons

Aprons are fun, functional, and easy to sew. Make one that matches your kitchen, or recycle an old party dress so that you can feel fancy and flouncy when you're hard at work.

BEGINNERS' LUCK
This project is good for first-time seamsters.

Dressy Aprons

Grown out of a favorite flouncy dress? Or have you grown out of dresses altogether?
The pretty floral frocks in your closet make great aprons for kitchen, garden, or studio.

1. Lay dress flat on table or floor.

2. For a half-apron, cut dress at the waist, all the way around.

3. For a full apron, cut off the sleeves and cut off the back. If the dress already has a sash, leave it intact.

4. For a finished look, pin sides and then hem by hand or machine.

5. Add ties as needed. A half apron needs a tie at top right and top left.

6. A full apron needs ties at the top and at the sides.

MORE IDEAS • Having an art or cooking party? Aprons make great party favors, and your guests will go home clean. • Decorate plain white aprons with fabric markers, paints, or crayons. • Have fun with these apron games: playing restaurant, playing hotel, playing house.

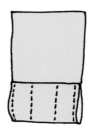

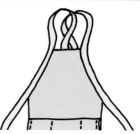

Dish Towel Apron

1. Lay towel flat.

2. Trim off two corners from top.

3. To make pockets, fold up bottom and stitch up sides. Stitch two lines in the middle to divide into three pockets.

4. To make ties, cut two lengths of grosgrain ribbon (about 50 inches each). Pin along each angled edge so that a piece hangs out at the top and the middle on each side. Sew along the edge.

Tube Skirts

Project designed by Joy Hayes

This basic skirt is easy to make—you don't even need a pattern. The design possibilities are endless as you put together stripes and layers of fabric.

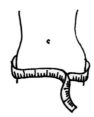

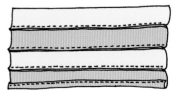

1. The first step is design! See what fabrics and trim you have, and make a sketch. Put together strips of fabric to create a banded skirt, or layer fabrics over each other for a dimensional effect.

2. Measure the width of your body around the hips. Your skirt has to be big enough to come up and down over the widest part of your body. Now, measure the length you want your skirt to be. Add an inch to both the length and the width for seams. Our design is 37 inches wide by 18 inches long.

3. Cut out strips of fabric to equal the total length (plus one inch), and sew them together. It's easy to make mistakes, so have an adult help you. Press the seams flat after sewing. Hem the bottom and add trim.

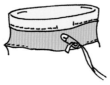

4. Sew the two ends together to make a tube.

5. Cut a piece of elastic that feels good around your waist, plus a few extra inches. Working from the inside of the skirt, fold over some fabric and sew it to make a pocket for the elastic. Leave an opening where you can insert the elastic.

6. Stick a safety pin through the elastic and push it through the pocket. Make sure you don't pull the end of the elastic all the way through, or you will have to start over! Sew the two ends of the elastic together firmly, by hand or on the sewing machine.

7. Turn skirt right-side-out and wear it!

Layered Skirt
Designed by Isabella, age 8

Striped Skirt
Designed by Ruby, age 7

Why We Wrote This Book

Design is not just for rainy days.

This book was written by a pair of identical twins. We are designers, writers, mothers, teachers, and citizens. We grew up in the 1960s and 70s in an intellectual household where typewriters outnumbered televisions. The "art box" was our favorite toy: a stash of markers, paints, and paper that led to the production of tiny books and magazines, our first adventures in self-publishing.

Now we are adults with our own careers and families. Ellen is a graphic designer and design educator, and Julia is an English professor. At work, we both use media in order to teach, write, and communicate. At home, we use our own art boxes—real and virtual—to make books, cards, invitations, Web sites, and T-shirts with our kids and their friends. In the process, our kids are learning to navigate the sea of images, products, and information that surrounds us all. They are taking the tools of marketing into their own hands in order to build their own visions of what's hip, cool, beautiful, and just.

We are not alone. Concerned adults and thoughtful kids across America are looking for alternatives to the visions of childhood packaged by consumer culture. D.I.Y. parents—adults with creative interests, technological know-how, and a sense of social responsibility—are raising D.I.Y. kids. These families are saying *no* to endless consumerism and *yes* to art, craft, and home-grown media. This book is for them. It is also for educators working in schools,

museums, camps, and after-school programs, as well as for aunts and uncles, friends and babysitters, neighbors and citizens—anyone who wants to create a better world for and with the next generation. Most of all, it is for kids who want to make their mark on the world.

D.I.Y. stands for "Do It Yourself." The D.I.Y. movement has touched not only the domestic arts but also graphic design, journalism, and publishing. This book is a sequel to *D.I.Y.: Design It Yourself*, a book written by Ellen and her graduate students at Maryland Institute College of Art. While she was working on the first book, we realized that raising kids is the ultimate D.I.Y. activity: no matter how much you read or how many people try to help you, you are ultimately alone, faced with the terrible splendor of your child's singularity. You make decisions as best you can in a world defined by school, work, and mass media. We believe that design can help.

Design is more than the stuff you buy at high-end stores, or the modern look that moves products at Target and IKEA. Design is a practice, a way of presenting images and ideas to the various publics that make up your social world. Design can transform everything from homework to doodling into occasions for social, artistic, and verbal fun. Design thinking can help you evaluate your environment and your shopping cart in order to make choices that are smarter, better, and more

beautiful. Design is not just a profession or a hobby. Design is a life skill.

D.I.Y. families are increasingly treating their living spaces as studios rather than nests. Nesting, the domestic paradigm of the 1990s, implies a child-centered enclave insulated from the outside world by name-brand furnishings. The studios of the new millennium are open houses rather than closed ones, lively centers of sociability, communication, and work. The agenda includes everything from making gifts instead of buying them to staging memorable birthday parties and producing one's own media.

This book encourages a kind of play that has been edged out of households caught in the great Habitrail of soccer practice and homework. D.I.Y. projects may require a little initial supervision, but at their best they trigger imaginative play, without requiring fees, teams, or the minivan.

The projects in *D.I.Y. Kids* rely primarily on ready-to-hand supplies, not corporate kits or systems. Most activities involve physical, hands-on making, but some include tips for working with digital tools. Most projects make a minimal mess: we prefer pencils, markers, and tape to paint and papier mache. Finally, kids should be able to do most of the work themselves.

There are many arts and crafts guides for kids. None of them emphasizes design. The projects in our book introduce design concepts, such as patterns, icons, logos, and lettering. Other projects feature objects that function or communicate, such as books, zines, T-shirts, and party supplies. Most of the projects in this book are illustrated with actual work by actual kids.

D.I.Y. Kids is driven by a philosophy. We aim to teach design literacy to anyone who will listen— kids, parents, teachers, friends. Design literacy means understanding design from the inside, as producers of images, not just consumers. In the twenty-first century, being in the audience is not enough. D.I.Y. kids (and the adults who care about them) want to build their world, not just sit and watch.

As identical twins, we grew up finishing each other's sentences. It only makes sense that we are now finishing each other's book. We relied on our kids and their friends to make the art featured here. We got to be curators, art directors, and project managers; they provided the creative talent. Sometimes, they followed our directions. Other times, they came up with their own work to do. We couldn't have produced the book without them. *D.I.Y. Kids* is dedicated to our children: Ruby and Jay Miller, and Hannah, Isabel, Lucy, and Eliot Reinhard.

— *Ellen and Julia Lupton*